SPANI

IN

C000184416

Order with confidence when
in Spain

Spanish - English
Menulator

Including Catalan

Throughout the menulater all Catalan words
and phrases are identified with an asterisk

Throughout this book you will find several
"Tips and Helpful Phrases"

You may find it useful to read these before using
the dictionary section

For Special diets please see
Tips and Helpful Phrases on page 60

Introduction

Catalan words and phrases in this menulator are identified with an asterisk. Barcelona is the capital of Catalonia

When entering a restaurant in Spain you will generally wait to be seated:
Greet the waiter with **Hola** followed by:
cuatro (4) personas por favor
quatre (4) personas si us plau*
A table for 4 people please.

Manners are important in Spain:
por favor
Si us plau*
please,
Gracias / Muchas gracias
Gràcies* / Moltes gràcies*
Thank you

They may ask for your drinks order:
la bebida?, per beure?
un aperitiu*
Possible answers: -
Un Agua Minera
Aigua mineral*
Mineral water
Sin Gas
Sense gas*
Still water
Con Gas
Amb gas*
Sparkling water
Un Té
Te*
Tea

Possible answers cont: -

Un Café Solo
Café sol*
Black coffee or Expresso

Un Descafeinado
Descafeïnat*
Decaffeinated

Un Café con leche
Café amb Llet* *(pronounced 'yet')*
White coffee

Un vaso de Leche
Llet* *(pronounced 'yet')*
Milk

Una copa de Vino Tinto
Vinegre*
Red wine

Una copa de Vino Rosado
Vi rosat*
Rosé wine

Una copa de Vino Blanco
Vi blanc*
White wine

Una Cerveza
Cervesa*
A bottle of beer

Ginebra
Gin

Botella
Ampolla*
Bottle

Zumo
Suc*
Juice

Sangría
Chilled red wine with lemonade and citrus fruit

Meals and eating times

El desayuno
Esmorzar*
Breakfast 07:00–10:00

La comida o el almuerzo,
Dinar*
Lunch 13:00 – 15:30

La cena
Sopar*
Dinner 21:00 – 00:00

You should have **el menú / la carta** by now
(Incidentally, menus are generally displayed outside the
restaurant with prices)

The menu may be presented as follows: -

Primero, Entremeses, Ensaladas y Sopa,
Entremeses,
Amanidas i sopa*
Starters, salads and soups

Segundo Second course can be displayed on
smaller menus but other courses may be
displayed as follows :-

Verduras, Huevos, Pastas y Arroces,
Verdures
Ous, pasta I arrossos*
Vegetables, egg dishes, pasta and rice dishes

Pescados y Mariscos
Peix i marisc*
Fish and seafood

Carnes
Carns*
Meat and main dishes

Postres, Pastelería, Helados, Frutas y Quesos,
Postres, pastisseria, gelateria
Fruita i formatges*
Desserts, pastries, ice creams, fruits and cheeses

Menú del dia

Fixed price menu of the day

e.g.: -
2 Platos, postre y bebida
2 Plats, postre i beguda*
2 courses, dessert and drink

These menus are a great way of simplifying the whole ordering process.

The waiter will ask you
Que vol, qué quiere tomar?
Prendre?*
What will you have?

You then have to indicate to the waiter whether you are choosing a fixed price menu
e.g. **Menú del día** or **la carta**

Sometimes you will get a special menu

e.g **MENÚ PRESTIGE** which is a selection of a number of small plates of local items, enough for the whole table.

At the end of each course the waiter will say
Han Terminado?
Have you finished

After the meal

La Cuenta, por favor
Elcompte sí us plau*
The bill please.

Servicio incluido
Servei inclòs*
Service charge included, but small coins given in
change are usually left in any event. If there is
a note saying **servicio no incluido** then
between 5% and 10% is standard. The bill will include
IVA value added tax

On leaving the restaurant: -
Muchas gracias
Moltes gràcies*
Adiós
Adéu*
Thank you very much, goodbye

TAPAS served in bars. Highly recommended for tourists
and as a good introduction to Spanish
food. Tapas dishes are something to pick at or
eat when having a drink or you can order 2 or
3 tapas per person to have a light meal or
snack. There are usually 2 prices – one for
sitting at the bar and another higher price for
sitting at a table. Tapas are a small version of
main dishes.

RACIONES
These are larger versions of Tapas.

A To
A la parilla / plancha Grilled
A la romana Fried in batter
Abadeig* Pollack
Abadejo Pollack
Abanico Something displayed on a plate
Abierto Open
Abuela Traditional like grandma makes
Acedera Sorrel
Acedias fritas Fried baby sole
Aceite de oliva Olive oil
Aceite girasol Sunflower oil
Aceitunas Olives
Aceitunas rellenas Stuffed olives
Acelga Beet tops (similar to spinach)
Achicoria Chicory
Àcid* Tangy
Ácida Tangy
Aceite Oil
Acido Tangy
Acompanyament* Garnish
Acompañamiento Garnish
Aderezo de mesa Condiments
Aderezo Dressing
Adob* Marinade / Season
Adobado(a) Marinated
Adobat* Marinated
Adobo Marinade / Season
Adorn* Dressing
Afegir* To add
Agre* Sour / Bitter
Agredolçe* Sweet and sour
Agrella* Sorrel

Agrest* Wild
Agreste Wild
Agridulce Sweet and sour
Agrio Sour / bitter
Agua Water
Aguacate Avocado
Aguadiente Strong liquor
Aguamiel Honey sauce
Aguaturma Jerusalem artichoke
Aguayon Rump
Aguja Gar or needlefish
Agujas para cocinar Boiling beef
Agujas, en On skewers
Agulat* Rock salmon
Agulla* Gar or needlefish
Ahir* Yesterday
Ahumado Smoked
Ahumados surtidos Plate of smoked meats
Aigua* Water
Aiguamel* Honey sauce
Aiguardents* Strong liquor
Aixafar* To crush
Ajedrea Spring garlic
Ajetes Fried garlic
Ají Chilli pepper
Ajiaceite Garlic and oil sauce
Ajillo White wine and garlic/ garlic and
olive oil
Ajitos Chopped garlic
Ajo (s) Garlic
Ajo blanco Chilled almond and garlic soup
Ajoarriero Hot garlic sauce with tomatoes
and peppers

Al Ajillo In garlic
Al Forn* Baked, roasted
Al horno Baked, roasted
Al To the
Ala (s) Wing(s)
Alajú* Small round cakes
Albacora Swordfish
Albahaca Basil
Albaricoques Apricots
Albeca* White of an egg
Albercoc* Apricot
Alberginas a la catalan Fried aubergine cooked in tomato sauce
Alberginas farcits* Stuffed aubergines with beef, garlic breadcrumbs and egg, sometimes with fish.
Alberginia* Aubergine
Albóndigas Meat balls, faggots
Albondiguitas Small meat balls
Albor* Small bream
Alboronia* Samfaina (assorted vegetables aubergines, garlic and olive oil)
Albura White of an egg
Alcachofas Artichokes
Alcachofas salteadas Artichokes (sautéed)
Alcaparras Capers
Alcaravea Caraway seeds
Alcaravia* Caraway seeds
Alcorza Icing
Alfàbrega* Basil
Alfajores Small round cakes
Alfóncigo Pistachio nut

Alga Marina Seaweed
Algo Something displayed on a plate
Alguno Some / any
Aliñada (o) Vinaigrette
Aliño Simple vinaigrette
Aliño de atún Tuna with vinaigrette
Aliño de gambas Prawn with vinaigrette
Aliño de pulpo Octopus with paprika
Alioli* Garlic and oil sauce
Alitas (de pollo) Fried chicken wings
All i pebre* Garlic and pepper
All tender* Fried garlic
All(s)* Garlic
Almadraba Place near Alicante
Almadrote Sauce of mashed garlic and
hard cheese
Almejas Clams
Almejas a la marinera Clams in wine and
parsley
Almejas naturals lIve clams
Almendra Almond
Almendras, tostadas Toasted almonds
Almíbar Syrup
Almívar. Syrup
Almuerzo Lunch
Alt. High
Alto High
Altre* Other
Alubias Haricot beans
Alvocat* Avocado
Amanida Catalana* Mixed salad with cold
meats and hard boiled egg
Amanida de areng* Herring salad

Amanida de gambas* Prawn salad
Amanida de horta* Farm salad
Amanida de rúcula* Rocket salad
Amanida rus* Russian salad (potatoes, mayonnaise, carrots and peas)
Amanida tebi* Warm salad
Amanida Valencia* Valencian salad
Amanida* Salad
Amaniment de gambas* Prawns with vinaigrette
Amaniment de toninya* Tuna with vinaigrette
Amaniment* Relish
Amanit* Vinaigrette
Amaranto Amaranth
Amarg* Bitter
Amargo Bitter
Amarilla, en Sauce made from onions, saffron, and thickened egg yolks
Amb* With
Ametlla* Almond
Ametlles* Almonds
Amontillado Spanish white sherry
Ampolla* Bottle
Anacard* Cashews
Anacardos Cashews
Añadir To add
Ananá* Pineapple
Ancas de rana Frogs legs
Anchoas Anchovies
Andaluz, salsa Andalucian sauce
Anditos Black pudding with onion
Andrajos Casserole with pasta squares, meat or fish

Ànec (ànega)* Duck (female duck)
Anega* Potato stew
Añejo Aged /old
Anet Dill
Angelot* Angel fish /small shark
Angelote Angel fish/small shark
Anguila Eel
Angulas Baby eels
Anis Aniseed
Anona Custard apple
Antic* Old
Antigua Old
Antojito Tortilla filled with meat, tomatoes and onions
Anxova* Anchovies
Anyell* Lamb
Aperitivo Aperitif
Api* Celery
Apio Celery
Apio-nabo Celeriac
Araña* Weever fish (for soup)
Arándano Billberry/ blueberry
Aranger* Grapefruit
Aranya* Weever fish (for soup)
Ardilla Squirrel
Arencas Salted sardines
Areng* Herring
Arenque Herring
Arnadi Pumpkin, sugar and pine nut cake
Aroma del bosque Forest herbs
Arrebossa* Fried in batter
Arriero Country style

Arriero Country style
Arrissat* Curl
Arròs a escollir* Rice to choose
Arròs amb llet* *(pronounced 'yet')* Rice pudding
Arròs negre* Rice with squid ink
Arròs salvatge* Wild rice
Arròs* Rice
Arroz Rice
Arroz a banda Valencian Fish and rice dish. The rice, flavoured with saffron and fish stock is served first. The fish which were cooked in the stock is then served. (separate)
Arroz a escoger Rice to choose
Arroz a la alicantina Fish stew with pepper, garlic, artichoke hearts and saffron
Arroz a la valenciana Rice with seafood
Arroz con Leche Rice pudding
Arroz negro Rice with squid ink
Arroz salvaje Wild rice
Artejo Knuckle
Artell* Knuckle
Artesà* Home style
Artesano Home style
Arveja Peas
Asado Roast
Asados Roasted
Asopao Rice stew with meat or fish
Assortit d'embotits* Assorted cold sausage and salami
Assortit de formatges* Cheese board / platter

Assortit* Platter /assortment
Atemperada Temperature
Atún Tuna
Au* Fowl /chicken
Ave Fowl /chicken
Avellana Hazelnut
Avestruz Ostrich
Àvia* Traditional like "Grandma makes"
Aviram Poultry / fowl
Avui* Today
Azafrán Saffron
Azahar Orange blossom
Azúcar Sugar
Azul Blue

Tips & Helpful Phrases

Del día
Of the day (today)

Del país
Local

De la casa
Of the house

Bacalao Cod
Bacalao a la vizcaína Cod served with ham peppers and chilli's
Bacalao al pil pil Cod served with chilli's and garlic
Bacallà al pil pil* Cod served with chilli's and garlic
Bacallà* Cod
Bacon Bacon
Bacora Swordfish
Badia* Bay
Baguetines Small rolls
Bahía Bay
Baix* Low
Bajo Low
Bajoques farcides Red peppers stuffed with rice and meat or cod
Baldana Black pudding
Banda Group, band or style
Bandarillo Cocktail stick with bits of cheese and ham.
Bandeja Tray
Barbacoa Barbeque
Barbada Brill
Barbate Tuna from Barbate
Barquillos Biscuit rolls
Barra de pan Loaf of bread / baguette
Barreja* Blend, mixture or medley
Barrita Bread fingers
Bartolillos Triangles filled with custard then deep fried
Basca* Basque style
Batata Sweet potato

Batido Milkshake
Batidor Whisk
Batut* Milkshake
Bayetón Bubble and squeak with bacon
Bé* Good
Be* Sheep
Beacon Bacon
Bebidas Drinks
Becadas Woodcock
Bechamel White sauce
Begudas* Drinks
Beicon Bacon
Beicón Breakfast bacon
Beina* Pod
Beixamel* White sauce
Bellota Acorn
Ben fet* Well done
Berberechos Cockles
Berejenas a la catalana Fried aubergines cooked in tomato sauce
Berenar* Afternoon snack
Berenjena Aubergine (eggplant)
Berenjenas rellenas Stuffed aubergines with beef, garlic, breadcrumbs and egg
Berro Watercress
Bertón Stuffed cabbage
Berza Green cabbage
Bescuit* Sponge finger
Besuc blanc al forn Baked sea bream
Besuc blanc* Sea bream
Besugo al horno Baked sea bream
Besuc blanc* Sea bream
Besugo al horno Baked sea bream

Besugo Sea bream
Betabel Beet
Beure* To drink
Bien Good
Bienmesabe (fish course) Marinated fish
Bienmesabe (desert) Sweet ground
almonds and cinamon
Bigarro Winkle
Bikini Toasted cheese and ham sandwich
Bilbaína Basque style
Bisbe blanc / negre* Black pudding
Biscote French toast
Biscuit Biscuit
Bisque Creamy soup
Bistec Steak
Bistec de ternera Veal steak
Bistec de vedella Veal steak
Bizcocho (s) Sponge finger
Bizkaina a la Onion and tomato red sauce
used on fish
Blanc* White
Blancas White (beans)
Blanco White
Blando Soft / mild / bland
Blat de moro Corn / maize
Blat* Wheat
Blau* Blue
Bleda* Beet tops (similar to spinach)
Boca Mouth
Bocadillo Sandwich on a crusty white
bread roll
Bocas Seafood / crab claws

Bogovante Lobster
Bol Bowl
Bola Croquette
Bolet d'espinacal* Oyster mushrooms
Bolet* Wild mushrooms
Boleto Cep mushroom
Bolets amb pernil Cep mushrooms and ham
Bolets* Wild mushrooms
Boletus Type of mushroom
Bollo Sweet bun
Boloñesa vegetariana Vegetarian bolognaise
Bomba helada Baked Alaska
Bomba Meatball with chilli sauce
Bombón (es) Chocolate (s)
Boniato Sweet potato
Bonito Tuna
Bonito al horno Baked tuna fish
Bonito con tomate Tuna with tomato
Bonítol al forn* Baked tuna
Bonítol amd tomàquet* Tuna with tomato
Bonítol* Tuna
Boqueron (es) Fresh anchovy (ies)
Boquitas Small crab claws
Borona Cornmeal bread
Borra Salted cod and potato soup
Borracho Grey gurnard fish
Borrachos, Borrachuelos Doughnuts or cakes soaked in wine or syrup
Borraja Green vegetable (used in a stews)
Borratxo* Red gurnard

Borregos Cumin flavoured biscuits
Borró* Salted cod and potato soup
Bosc* Wood / forest
Bosque Wood / forest
Botella Bottle
Botifarra Catalan sausage
Botifarra amb Mongetes* Catalan sausage
with beans
Botifarra negre* Black pudding
Botifarró* Black pudding
Bou estofat* Beef stew
Bou* Beef / bull
Bover* A large edible snail
Braceado Grilled
Brandada de bacalao Creamed cod puree
with potatoes and garlic
Braó Pork shank
Braó* Cut of meat from the shoulder
Brasa Hot coal (char grilled)
Brasea To braise
Braseada (os) Braised
Bravas Fried potatoes in a spicy tomato
sauce
Brawni Brownie
Brazo de gitano Creamy cake roll
Brazuelo Cut of meat from the shoulder
Breca Small bream
Brécol Broccoli
Brettone Brussel sprouts
Brevas Figs
Brindis A toast for drinking
Broa Biscuits

Brocheta Kebab, skewer
Bróculi* Broccoli
Broqueta de riñones Kidney kebabs
Broqueta* Kebab, skewer (tapa)
Brotes Sprouts or bean sprouts
Brou* Broth
Bru* Brown
Bruneta Type of mushroom (Catalan)
Budín inglés Fruit cake
Bueno Good
Buey Beef / bull
Buey de mar Large crab
Bufé Buffet
Bull* Spiced ham
Bullbesa Fish soup
Bullbessa* Fish soup
Bullir* Boil / simmer
Bullit Mallorcan stew
Bunyettes Yeast doughnuts
Bunyols* Warm sugared deep fried doughnut
Buñuelos Light fried pastries
Buñuelos de viento Choux pastry
Buñuelos Fried choux pastry
Burato Crepe
Burger Hamburger
Burgos Soft fresh cheese
Burritos Stuffed tortillas
Búsano Whelk
Butifarra Catalana Catalan spicy sausage
Butifarra con judias Catalan sausage with beans
Butifarra somalla Tender cured sausage

Caballa Mackerel
Cabdell* Cabbage
Cabdell* Lettuce heart
Cabeces Heads (garlic)
Cabeza de cordero Lambs head
Cabirol Roe deer
Cabra Goat
Cabracho Scorpion fish
Cabrales Creamy blue cheese
Cabreig de mar* Rock fish
Cabreta Kid
Cabrilla (o) Rock fish
Cabriota asado Roast kid / goat
Cabrit* Kid / goat
Cabrito Kid / goat
Caça* Game
Caçado* Hunter style cooking
Cacao en polvo Cocoa
Cacau* Cocoa
Cacauet* Peanuts
Cacauetes Peanuts
Cacerola Pan (sauce pan)
Cachelada Pork stew with eggs, tomato and onion
Cachelos Type of potato (Galician)
Cadira* Chair
Cafè amb gel* Iced coffee
Cafè amb llet* *(pronounced 'yet')* Coffee with plenty of milk. Hot or cold.
Café Americano Black coffee
Café con hielo Iced coffee

Café con leche Coffee with milk
Café cortado Espresso with a drop of milk
Cafè sol* Black espresso
Café solo Black espresso
Cailón Shark
Caixa* Cashier
Cajero Cashier
Calabacín Courgette
Calabacines Zucchini, courgette
Calabaza Pumpkin
Calamar (es) Squid(s)
Calamar (es) en su tinta Squid cooked in its ink
Calamares a la romana Fried squid
Calamarsets farcits* Stuffed squid
Calamarset* Small squid
Calanda Herbs
Calçots* Type of spring onions
Calderada Fish soup
Caldereta Stew
Caldereta gallega Vegetable stew
Caldero Cooking pot
Caldillo Gravy
Caldo a la taza Cup of clear soup
Caldo con yema Meat broth with egg yolk
Caldo gallego Soup stew with beans, vegetables
and ham bone
Caldo* Broth
Caldosa Rice soup
Calent* Hot / warm
Càlid* Warm
Caliente Hot

Callampa Type of mushroom
Callos a la madrileña Tripe cooked with chilli's
Callos Tripe
Calvados Drink made from apples
Cama* Leg / thigh
Cambrer (a)* Waitress (er)
Camarera (o) Waitress (er)
Camarón Prawns
Camote Sweet potato
Camp* Countryside
Campo Countryside
Caña Stem / Stalk / cane sugar
Caña Cut of meat
Caña Small beer
Caña Straw
Caña de dulce / chocolate Puff pastry finger
with custard / chocolate filling
Caña de lomo iberica Cured loin of ham
Caña de vaca Marrow bone
Caña grande Large beer
Canalones Cannelloni pasta
Canela Cinnamon
Canelón Cannelloni
Cangrejo aliñado Dressed crab
Cangrejo Crab
Cangrejos del rio Freshwater crayfish
Canonge* Salad
Canóngio Salad
Cansalada Bacon
Cansalada* Bacon
Cantàbric* Cantabrian style
Cantábrico Cantabrian style

Cañas rellenas Custard rolls
Canya de llom ibèric* Cured loin of ham
Canya* Small beer
Canya* Stem / stalk / sugar cane
Canyella* Cinnamon
Cap de Xai* Lambs head
Cap i pota* Stewed calf's head and foot
Cap* Head
Capa Layer / cover
Capuccino White frothy coffee
Car* Expensive
Carabinero Large shrimp
Caracoles Snails
Caracolillos Small snails
Caramel-listar* Caramelized
Caramelizadas Caramelized
Caramelizado Caramelized
Caramelo Caramel
Carbassa* Pumpkin
Carbassó* Courgette
Carboná Cooked over coals
Carbonada Cooked over coals
Carbonitzada* Cooked over coals
Cardamomo Cardamom
Cardo Thistle
Careta de cerdo Pigs cheek
Cargolets* Small snails
Cargoli Winkle
Cargols* Snails
Cari Curry

Carn amb salsa de tomàquet* Meat in tomato sauce
Carn de bou* Beef
Carn de Cavall* Horsemeat
Carn de Vedella*Veal
Carn freda* Cold meat
Carn picada* Minced meat
Carn rustida* Round steak
Carn seca i salada* Dried beef eaten raw
Carn* Meat
Carne Meat
Carne a la Castellana Meat served with tomatoes, potato croquettes and onion rings
Carne de buey Beef
Carne de caballo Horsemeat
Carne de ternera Veal
Carne de venado Venison
Carne en salsa de tomate Meat in tomato sauce
Carne para asar Round steak
Carne picada Minced meat
Carnero Mutton
Carneros Mutton
Caro Expensive
Carpa Carp
Carpaccio Thin slices of meat / fish
Carquinyolis* Almond biscuits
Carrabiner* Large shrimp
Carril Rocket
Carrillada de cerdo Pork cheek
Carrilleras Cheek

Carro de queso Cheese board
Carta Menu / list
Carxofer* Artichokes
Casa (de la) House (of the)
Casados Meat cooked with rice, beans and vegetables
Cáscara Shell / peel
Casero (as) Homemade
Casolà (ana)* Homemade
Cassatta Napolitana Italian ice cream
Casserola* Pan (saucepan)
Cassola* Saucepan
Cassoulet Homemade
Castaña Chestnut
Castanya* Chestnut
Castanyola* Bream
Cava Spanish sparkling wine
Caza Game
Cazadora Hunter style cooking
Cazallera (o) Style of cooking
Cazón Dogfish
Cazuela Casserole
Ceba* Onion
Cebiche Raw fish marinated in lemon
Cebolla Onion
Cebolletas Spring onion
Cebollinos Chives
Cebón Young pork
Cecina de vaca Smoked-dried beef
Cecina Dried beef eaten raw
Centeno Rye
Centollo Spider crab

Centro Centre
Cep* Vine
Cepa Vine
Cerdo Pork
Cereales Cereal (breakfast)
Cerebro Brains
Cereza (s) Cherry (ies)
Cerrado Closed
Cerro Neck / Backbone
Cervell* Brains
Cervesa* Beer
Cerveza Beer
Cérvol Deer
Cesta de Frutas Fruit basket
Cesta Fabiola Style of fabiola (desert)
Cesta Basket
Cestina de Chantilly Wafer biscuit with chantilly
Cestita Little basket
Ceviche Raw fish marinated
Chabacano Apricot
Chacinas Collection of cold meats
Chafada Flattened / pressed
Chafar To crush
Chalote Shallot
Chambaret Hind shank
Chambarete de mano Fore shank
Champiñón a la crema Mushrooms with cream sauce
Champiñón al ajillo Garlic mushrooms
Champiñones Mushrooms

Chanfaina Sauce with tomatoes, peppers, onions and aubergine
Chanquetes Fish similar to whitebait
Chateaubriand Fillet of beef
Chato Glass of wine
Chícharo (s) Pea (s)
Chicharrones Crackling fried pork pieces
Chigró Chickpea
Chili Chilli
Chilindron Red pepper and tomato sauce with garlic and olives
Chipirones Squid
Chipirones rellenos Stuffed squid
Chirimoya Custard apple
Chirivia Parsnip
Chirlas Clams
Chispeado Sprinkled
Chistora Spicy sausage
Chocha Woodcock
Choco (s) Cuttle fish
Chocolate a la taza Thick chocolate sauce
Chopitos Small stuffed squids
Chorizo Cold spicy sausage
Chucho Doughnut filled with custard
Chucrut Sauerkraut
Chuleta de aguayon Sirloin steak
Chuleta de buey Beef chop
Chuleta de cerdo Pork chop
Chuleta de cerdo empanada Breaded pork chop
Chuleta de cordero Lamb chop
Chuleta de dos lomos Porterhouse steak
Chuleta Chop

Chuleta de ternera Veal chop
Chuletas Chops
Chuletitas Suckling pork chops
Chuletón T bone steak
Chumichurri BBQ sauce from Argentina
Chuny Chutney
Churrasco Charcoal grilled meat
Churros Fried pastry / dough cut into lengths covered in sugar
Cielo Sweet custard desert
Ciervo Deer, venison
Cigala Dublin Bay prawn / crayfish
Cigalitas Prawns
Cigar* Cigar
Cigrons* Chickpeas
Cilandro Coriander
Cinc* Five
Cinco Five
Cireres* Cherry (ies)
Ciruela Plum
Ciruelas pasas Prunes
Cistella de fruitas Fruit basket
Cítric* Citrus
Cítrico Citrus
Citries Citrus
Civada* Oats
Civil Civil
Clandestí* Secret
Clandestino Secret
Clara* Egg white
Clatell* Nape of the neck
Claus* Cloves

Clavo de olor Cloves
Clavos Cloves
Clemencia Small orange
Cloïses* Clams
Closca* Shell / peel
Coca mallorquina Savoury pastry
Coca* Sponge cake
Cochifrito Deboned lamb,onion,garlic,
paprika and parsley
Cochinillo Suckling pig
Cocidas Hot pot
Cocido Stew / cooked
Cocido madrileño Meat stew with sausage
and chickpeas
Cocido Stew
Cocina Cooking
Coco Coconut
Cocochas Triangular cheek pieces of hake
Coco rallado Desiccated coconut
Coco ratllat* Desicated coconut
Cocohas Triangular throat pieces of hake
Cóctel de gambas Shrimp cocktail
Cóctel de mariscos Seafood cocktail
Codillo Pork shank
Codornices con uvas Quail cooked with
grapes
Condoniz Quail
Codony* Quince
Cogollo (s) Lettuce hearts
Cogollos de tudela Lettuce heart
Cogombre petit* Gherkin

Cogombre* Cucumber
Cogote Nape of the neck
Cohombro de mar Sea cucumber
Col de Bruselas Brusels sprout
Col* Cabbage
Cola de toro Ox tail
Cola Tail
Coles de Bruselas Brussel sprouts
Coliflor Cauliflower
Colinabo Turnip
Collita* Harvest / recently harvested
Colom Pigeon
Colores Colours
Coltell Knife
Comarca Region / area
Comedor Dining room
Complert* Complete / full
Completo Complete / full
Compota Jam
Compota de fruta Stewed fruit
Con almendras With almonds
Con crema With cream
Con With
Concha Shell
Concha Rolled flank steak
Conejo encebollado Rabbit served with
  onion
Conejo Rabbit
Confitado Preserved
Confitat (amb vinagre)* Pickle
Confitat* Preserved
Confitura Jam

Congre* Conger eel
Congrio Conger eel
Conil Style of Conil (Cadiz)
Conill* Rabbit
Cono Cone
Conquilla* Shell
Consomé Thin soup
Consomé d'au* Chicken soup
Consomé de ave Chicken soup
Contas (South American) Tapas
Contessa Ice cream cake
Continuación Continuation
Copa de helado Ice cream scoop
Copa Cup or glass
Copos de Avena Oats
Coquina Seafood (clam)
Cor* Heart
Corazón Heart
Corbina* Meagre (fish)
Corcho Cork
Cordero Chilindrón Lamb stew with onion, tomato peppers and eggs
Cordero Lamb
Cordobés Rolled stuffed ham from Cordoba
Corinto Sultana / raisin
Corriente Current / local
Cortado Sour milk
Corteza Crust / rind
Coruña Style from Coruña
Corva Cheek
Corvina Meagre (fish)

Corzo Roe deer
Cosechas Harvest / recently harvested
Cost* Price
Costa Coast
Costat* Side
Coste, Costo Price
Costella de porc* Pork chop
Costella de vedella* Veal chop
Costella* Chops
Costillas Ribs
Costillas de cerdo Pork ribs
Costra Crust / rind
Coulis Sauce of puréed fruit
Cranc del riu* Freshwater crayfish
Cranc* Large crab
Cranca* Spider crab
Crapaudine Butterflied and flattened
Créixens* Watercress
Crema Cream / custard
Crema ágria sour cream
Crema catalana Crème Brulée
Crema de cangrejos Cream of crab soup
Crema de cranc* Cream of crab soup
Crema del día Soup of the day
Crema para batir Whipping cream
Cremada* Sweet made with egg, sugar
and milk
Cremat* Toasted / burnt / flamed
Cremosa (o) Creamy
Creps Crepes
Criadillas Testicles, beef or lamb breaded
and fried in oil

Crocanti Italian ice cream with almonds
Croqueta* Croquette
Croquetas de pescado Fish cake
Croquetas Croquette
Croquetitas Small croquettes
Crotón Croutons
Cru* Raw
Crudo Raw
Crujiente Crunchy / crusty
Cruixent* Crunchy / crusty
Cua* Tail
Cuajada (os) Curd pudding
Cuatro Four
Cuchara Spoon
Cuchillo Knife
Cuina* Cooking
Cuit* Stew / cooked
Cuixa* Leg.thigh
Culantro Coriander
Culata de contra Knuckle, shin
Cullera* Spoon
Cullereta* Teaspoon
Curado Cured
Curat* Cured
Curri Curry
Cúspide Top / apex

USEFUL NOTES:

_____
_____
_____
_____
_____

Dadoitos Diced ham
Dado (s) Dice
Dasca Corn
Data* Date
Dátil Dates
Dàtil* Dates
Daurat* Bream
De Of / from
Debajo Under
Deditos Diced ham
Degustació* Sampling / tasting
Degustación Sampling / tasting
Del día Of the day
Del país Local
Del Of the
Delicia Delight
Delicias Small tapa biscuit
Dels Of / from
Demà* Tomorrow
Desalado De-salted
Desayuno Breakfast
Descafeinado Decaffeinated
Descafeïnat* Decaffeinated
Deshuesado De-boned
Desossat* De-boned
Despojos Offal
Despulles* Offal
Deu* Ten
Diabético Diabetic
Diente de ajo Clove of garlic
Dietético Diet
Diez Ten
Dinar* Lunch
Disfrutar Enjoy

Divers* Enjoy
Diversos Variety
Doce Twelve
Docena Dozen
Dolç* Sweet
Donostiarra Basque town
Dónut Doughnut
Dorada Bream
Dorado Browned / golden
Dos Two
Dotze* Twelve
Dotzena* Dozen
Dry-sack Dry Sherry
Dulce Sweet
Dur* Hard
Durazno Peach
Duro Hard

Tips & Helpful Phrases

Catalan words are identified with an asterisk

Frio **Fred*** Cold	**Caliente** **Calent*** Hot
Primavera Spring	**Otoño** **Tardor*** Autumn
Verano **Estiu*** Summer	**Invierno,** **Hivern*** Winter

Eglefino Haddock
Ejotes Green beans
El compte* The bill
Elegir Choose / select
El marisc* The shellfish
El peix* The fish
Els* The / them
Embotits* Sausages / cold meats
Embuchado In a sausage / stuffed
Embutido Sausage and cold meats
Empanada Stuffed savoury pastry
Empanada gallega Pastry with tuna
Empanadilla Fish or meat pie
Empanadillas de carne Meat pastries
Empañado Breaded
Emparedado Sandwich
Emparedrat* Sandwich
Empedrat* Salad with salt cod or tuna
and beans
Emperador Swordfish
Encargo, por Made to order
Encàrrec* Made to order
Encebolladas With onions
Enciam* Lettuce
Encurtidos Pickle
Endibia* Endives (lettuce leaves)
Endivias Endives (lettuce leaves)
Enebro Juniper berry
Eneldo Dill
En escabeche Marinated with herbs

Ensaimada Spiral shaped bun filled with custard

Ensaimada mallorquina Spiral shaped bun sometimes filled with custard or sweet pumpkin strands cold

Ensalada Salad

Ensalada Catalana Mixed salad with cold meats and hard boiled egg

Ensalada condés House special salad

Ensalada de arenque Herring salad

Ensalada de atún Tuna salad

Ensalada de escabechados Marinated platter of fish or meat

Ensalada de gambas Prawn salad

Ensalada de la huerta Farm salad

Ensalada de rúcula Rocket salad

Ensalada espolón Tropical salad

Ensalada mixta Mixed salad

Ensalada templada Warm salad

Ensalada tíbia Warm salad

Ensalada Valenciana Valencian salad

Ensaladilla Rusa Russian salad (mayonnaise salad with potatoes, carrots and peas)

En salsa In sauce

Entelat* Breaded

Entera Whole

Entrante Starters

Entrants* Starters

Entrecot Prime rib steak

Entremés Hors d'oeuvre

Entremeses Starters

Entremeses varios Mixed starters
Entrepà* Sandwich on a crusty roll
Equilibrium Balance
Eriçó de mar* Sea urchin
Erizo de mar Sea urchin
Esbarzer* Blackberry
Escabechados de la casa Marinated in
house style
Escabechados Marinated in house style
Escabeche Marinated
Escabeche (s) Pickled / marinated
Escabex* Pickled / marinated
Escalfado Poached
Escalibada Baked vegetables
Escalope de ternera Veal escalope
Escalopine Small fillet / escalope
Escalunya* Shallot
Escama (s) Flake
Escamarlà* Dublin bay prawns
Escarola Type of chicory lettuce
Escogidas Chosen
Escollit* Chosen
Escopinya (vius) Clams (live)
Escopinya francesa* Sea food clam
Escopinya gravada* Cockles
Escopinya* Cockles
Escorça* Crust / rind
Escorpena Scorpion fish
Escórpora* Scorpion fish
Escudella* Catalan meat and vegetable soup
Escudella I carn d'olla* Broth with pasta
followed by boiled meat and vegetables

Escupiña Cockle
Esencia Essence
Esencia de vainilla Vanilla essence
Esgarraet Roast peppers and cod
Esmorzar* Breakfast
Espadilla Shoulder chop
Espadín a la toledana Kebab
Espadín Type of swordfish
Espaguetis Alsacianas Noodles (from Alsace)
Espaguetis Boloñesa Spaghetti Bolognese
Espaguetis Italiana Spaghetti
Espaguetis Napolitana Spaghetti in tomato
and herb sauce
Espaguetis Spaghetti
Espalda (ala) Halved and grilled
Espalda Shoulder
Espanyola* Spanish
Española Spanish
Esparces* Asparagus
Esparces amb mayonesa* Asparagus with
mayonnaise
Esparces amb pernil* Asparagus with ham
Espardenya* Sea cucumber
Espardenyes Sea cucumber
Esparracada* Ragged
Espárragos con jamón Asparagus with ham
Espárragos con mayonesa Asparagus with
mayonnaise
Espárragos trigueros Green asparagus
Espárragos Asparagus

Espatlla* Shoulder
Espècia* (s) Spice
Especial (es) Specialty
Especialidad de la casa House speciality
Especialitit de la casa* House speciality
Espeto Cooked on a spit
Espinacas Spinach
Espinacas a la andaluza Spinach with
pine nuts and raisins
Espinacas a la catalana Spinach with pine
nuts, ham and garlic
Espinas Fish bones
Espinazo de cerdo con patatas Pork stew
with potatoes
Espuma Mousse
Esqueixada de bacalao Catalan salt cod salad
Esqueixada de Bacallà Catalan salt cod salad
Esquirol* Squirrel
Estació* Season
Estación Season
Estellar Chop up
Estil* Style
Estilo Style
Estiu* Summer
Estofado de liebre Hare stew
Estofado de ternera Stewed steak
Estofado(s) Stew
Estofar Braise / stew
Estofat (s)* Stew (s)
Estoró* Tarrogon
Estragón Tarragon
Estrella de la casa Star of the house
Estruç. Ostrich
Esturió* Sturgeon
Esturión Sturgeon

Catalan phrases are identified with an asterisk

Quisiera un poco de leche
Voldria una mica de llet*
To ask for some milk

Quisiera un poco de mantequilla
Voldria una mica de mantega*
To ask for some butter

Quisiera un poco de sal
Voldria una mica de sal*
To ask for some salt

The word **llet** is
pronounced **"yet"**

USEFUL NOTES:

Faba* Broad bean
Fabada Bean stew with spicy sausage and black pudding
Fabada* Bean stew with spicy sausage and black pudding
Faisà* Pheasant
Faisán Pheasant
Faisán trufado Pheasant with truffles
Falda Saddle
Farcellets Herb bundells
Farcit* In a sausage / stuffed
Farigola Thyme
Farina* Flour
Farinetes Porridge
Farro Meat and vegetable soup
Favor , por Please
Feo Ugly
Fesol* French bean
Fesolet* French bean
Festival Festival
Fet (a)* Done
Fetge amb ceba* Liver cooked with onions
Fetge de pollastre* Chicken livers
Fetge de Vedella* Braised liver of veal
Fetge* Liver
Fiambres Cold meats
Fideos Small noodles, vermicelli
Fideu* Vermicelli / noodle
Fideuá Paella with pasta noodles
Fideuada Paella made with noodles
Figa Fig
Figaflor* Fig

Figues Figs
Filet* Sirloin
Filet a la graella* Grilled beef
Filet de vedella* Fillet of pork
File* Fillet steak
Filete a la parrilla Grilled beef
Filete de cerdo Pork steak
Filloas Large crêpe
Finas hierbas Fine herbs
Finas Fine
Flam al ron* Crème Caramel with rum
Flam amb nata* Crème Caramel with cream
Flam* Crème Caramel
Flama* Flambe
Flamenca (a la) Egg with sausage,
tomatoes and vegetables
Flan al ron Créme caramel with rum
Flan con nata Créme caramel with cream
Flan Créme caramel
Flauta* Large beer
Fleca* Bakery
Flequer* Baker
Flor de sal Flower of salt
Flor Flower
Fogassa* Loaf
Fogó Stove
Foie gras Duck paté
Foie Paté de foir
Fondue Arrangement of cooked meats
Fonoll* Fennel

Forca* Fork
Formatge amb codony* Cheese with quince jelly
Formatge blau* Blue cheese
Formatge de Burgos* Soft white cheese
Formatge de cabra* Goats cheese
Formatge d'ovella* Sheeps cheese
Formatge del pais* Local cheese
Formatge fregit* Fried cheese
Formatge manxego* Manchego cheese
Formatge* Cheese
Forn* Oven
Forquilla* Fork
Fort* Very spicy / strong
Fragancia Aroma
Frambuesa Raspberry
Frambuesas con nata Raspberries and cream
Francesa, a la French style
Freda* Cold
Fregit (ada)* Fry
Freír* Fry
Fréjol Beans
Fresa Strawberries
Fresas con nata Strawberries with cream
Fresca (s) Fresh
Fresón Large strawberry
Fricadelas Meat patties
Fricandó Pot roast, meat stew with wild mushrooms
Frijoles Beans
Frío (a) Cold
Fritada Fried dish

Fritada aragonesa Ratatouille
Fritada de pescado y marisco Fried fish and seafood platter
Fritas (os) Fried
Frito (s) Fried
Fritura de pescado Mixed fried fish
Fritura Fried food
Frituritas Mixed fried nibbles
Frixuelos Sweet pancakes
Fruita del mar* Shellfish
Fruita del temps* Fruit in season
Fruita en Almívar* Fruit in syrup
Fruita* Fruit
Fruta Fruit
Fruta de Aragón Chocolate coated crystallised fruit
Fruta de la pasión Passion fruit
Fruta del tiempo Fruit of the season
Fruta variada Assorted fresh fruit
Frutas del mar Shellfish
Frutas en almíbar Fruit in syrup
Frutos secos Dried fruits and nuts
Fuente Source / platter
Fuerte Very spicy / strong
Fuet Cured pork sausage
Fulles* Leaves
Fumar, no No smoking
Fumat* Smoked
Fumats (assortit)* Plate of smoked meats
Fundido Melted
Fusión Fusion

Gacha Orange coloured sauce with sausages
Gachas Porridge
Gaditana Style from Cadiz
Gajo(s) Segment(s)
Galera Shrimp
Galeta* Biscuit / wafer
Gall de mar John dory fish
Gall d'indí Turkey
Gall Grouse
Gall John dory fish
Gallega Galician style
Gallegues Galician style
Galleta Biscuit
Galletas de almendra Almond biscuit
Gallina Hen
Gallina de Guinea* Guinea fowl
Gallina en pepitoria Hen stewed with almonds and wine
Gallinejas Fried lambs intestines
Gallo de mar John Dory fish
Gallo Grouse
Galló* Segment
Galta de bou Cow's face
Galta* Cheek
Galtes de porc* Pigs cheek
Galtes Cutlets
Gamba Prawn
Gambas Shrimp / prawn
Gambas al ajillo Garlic prawns
Gambas al all* Garlic prawns

Gambas en gabardina Prawns in batter
Gambeta* Tiny prawns
Ganivet* Knife
Ganso Goose
Ganxet* Type of white bean
Garafa Carafe, decanter
Garbanzos Chickpeas
Garbanzos a la catalana Chickpeas with sausage, boiled eggs and pine seeds
Garrapiñadas sweetened almonds with caramel
Garrílletó* Suckling pig
Gaseosa Soda water
Gasosa* Soda water
Gaspatxo* Cold tomato and cucumber soup
Gaudir* Enjoy
Gazpacho Cold tomato and cucumber soup
Gazpacho andaluz Cold tomato and cucumber soup
Gazpacho Manchego Rich mixed game pâté
Gel* Ice
Gelat* Ice cream
Gelat de caramel* Caramel ice cream
Gelatina Jelly
Gelatinosa Gelatinized
Gelé de rúcula Rucola jelly
Gelea Jelly
Gelea* Jelly
Gemma* Egg yolk
Gerds amb nata* Raspberries with cream
Gerds* Raspberries

Germen* From wheat
Germinados Germinated
Gigot* Potted meat
Ginebre* Juniper berry
Gingebre* Ginger
Gla* Acorn
Glaç* Ice
Glacé Glazed
Glaseado (a) Omelette souflé
Globo Balloon
Globus* Balloon
Gnocchi Dumpling
Gofre Waffle
Got* Glass
Gotet de vi* Glass of wine
Gra* Grain / wheat
Gracias Thanks
Gràcies* Thanks
Gran Large
Granada Pomegranate
Granger* Farmers
Granissat* Sorbet drink
Granizado Sorbet drink
Granjeros Farmers
Grano Grain / wheat
Granollers Town in Catalonia
Granota* Frog
Grapat* A handful
Grasa Fat
Gratén Gratin
Gratinado Grilled
Gratinat* Grilled
Greix* Fat
Grelos Turnip tops

Grisín Bread stick
Grivia* Wrasse
Gros* Course / thick
Grosella Currant
Grosella blanca o verde Gooseberry
Grosella colorada Redcurrant
Grosella negra Blackcurrant
Grueso Coarse / thick
Grumo Lump
Grumoll* Lump
Guajolote Turkey
Guarnición Garnish
Guarnició* Garnish
Guatlles* Quail
Guayaba Guava
Guinda Cocktail or glacé cherry
Guinder / cirerer* Cocktail or glacé cherry
Guindilla Red chilli
Guisado Casserole
Guisado de cordero Lamb stew
Guisantes Peas
Guisat de Bacallà* Creamed cod puree
with potatoes and garlic
Guisat* Casserole
Guiso Stew
Gust* Taste
Gusto Taste / flavour

Habanero Very hot chilli pepper
Habas Broad beans
Habichuelas Beans
Habitas Broad beans
Hamburguesa* Hamburger
Harina Flour
Hecho (a) Done
Helado Ice cream
Helado de caramelo Caramel ice cream
Hervido Poached
Hervir Boil
Hielo Ice
Hierba Luisa Lemon verbena
Hierbabuena Mint
Higaditos de pollo Chicken livers
Hígado Liver
Hígado con cebolla Liver cooked with onions
Hígado de ternera estofado Braised liver
of veal
Higos Figs
Higos con miel y nueces Figs with honey
and nuts
Hinojo Fennel
Hipogloso Halibut
Hivern* Winter
Hogaza Loaf of bread
Hojaldre Puff pastry
Hojaldre clunia Style of pastry
Hojas Leaves / layers
Hojas verdes Green salad leaves
Hola Hello
Hongos Wild mushrooms
Hora Hour

Horchata Tiger nut drink
Hornazo Baked Easter cake
Horneada lentamente Oven cooked slowly
Horno Oven baked
Horta* Market / farm
Hortalissa* Vegetables / garden produce
Hortaliza Vegetables / garden produce
Hoy Today
Huachinango Red snapper
Huerta Market, Farm
Hueso Bone
Huesos de santos Stuffed marzipan rolls
Huevas Egg / roe
Huevo cocido Boiled eggs
Huevo duro Hard boiled egg
Huevo frito Fried egg
Huevo hilado Egg yolk garnish
Huevo parte clara Egg white
Huevo parte yema Egg yolk
Huevos Egg
Huevos a la flamenca Fried eggs with ham,
tomato and vegetables
Huevos a la mallorquina Eggs with
sausage
Huevos a la riojana Eggs with chorizo
Huevos caseros Home style eggs
Huevos escalfados Poached eggs
Huevos con picadillo Eggs with minced
Spanish sausage
Huevos pasados por agua Soft boiled eggs
Huevos revueltos Scrambled eggs
Huevos revueltos con jamón Scrambled
eggs with ham
Hummus Humus

I* And
Ibèric* Iberian
Ibérico Iberian
Ibérico de bellota Iberian cured ham
Idiazábal Smoked ewe's milk cheese
Ijada Flank
Invierno Winter
Iogurt de fruita* Fruit yoghurt
Iogurt* Yoghurt
Isla Island

Tips & Helpful Phrases

Catalan words are identified with an asterisk

Frito
Fregit*, Ferrat*
Fried

Asado / Horneado
A l'ast rostit*
Roast

Ahumado
Fumat*
Smoked

Asado a la parrilla
A l'ast a la parilla*
Grilled

Cocido al vapor
Cuinat al vapor*
Steamed

Hervido
Bullit*
Boiled

Estofado
Estofat*
Stewed

Pochado
Escalfat*
Poached

Tips & Helpful Phrases

Catalan words are identified with an asterisk

		Catalan
1	uno	un*
2	dos	dos*
3	tres	tres*
4	cuatro	quatre*
5	cinco	cinc*
6	seis	sis*
7	siete	set*
8	ocho	vuit*
9	nueve	nou*
10	diez	deu*

USEFUL NOTES:

Jabalí Wild boar
Jaiba Crab
Jalapeño Hot green pepper
Jalea Jelly
Jamón Ham
Jamón con huevo hilado Ham with egg yolk garnish
Jamón de bellota Cured ham from acorn fed pig
Jamón de Guijuelo Guijuelo raw ham
Jamón de Jabugo Top quality spanish cured ham
Jamón de pato Duck ham
Jamón de Sajona Boiled / smoked ham
Jamón dulce Cold boiled ham
Jamón Ibérico Cured ham
Jamón Serrano Spanish cured ham
Jarabe Syrup
Jardinera (a la) With vegetables
Jarret* Shank
Jarrete Shank
Jarrete de cordero Lamb shank
Jengibre Ginger
Jeta Pork cheek
Jibia Cuttlefish
Jinete Horse rider
Jitomate Red tomato
Jocoque Buttermilk
Jònec* Steer / heifer
Jorn Day
Judía French bean

Judías blancas Haricot beans
Judías verdes a la Española Bean stew
Jugo (en su) in its own juice
Jugo de lima Lime juice
Jugo de limón Lemon juice
Jugoso Juicy
Julivert* Parsley

Tips & Helpful Phrases

Catalan words are identified with an asterisk

Un cuchillo
Un ganivet*
Knife
Un tenedor
Forquilla*
Fork
Una cuchara
Cullera*
Spoon

Un vaso
Got*
Glass
Una taza
Tassa*
Cup
Un cenicero
Cendrer*
Ashtray

Karrakelas Perrywinkles
Ketchup Ketchup
Kiskillas Prawns
Kiwi Kiwi
Kokotxas* (cocochas) Triangular cheek
pieces of hake

Tips & Helpful Phrases

Catalan words are identified with an asterisk

Del pan
Pa*
Bread

Mantequilla
Mantega*
Butter

Leche
Llet* *(pronounced 'yet')*
Milk

Sal
Salt

Un agua
Aigua*
Water

Por favour
Si us plau*
Please

Tips & Helpful Phrases

Catalan words and phrases are identified with an asterisk

Soy alérgico a los
Sóc al·lèrgic als*
I am allergic to......

Cacahuetes **Cacahuets*** Nuts	**Al trigo** **Blat*** Wheat	**Huevos** **Ous*** Eggs
Mariscos **Marisc*** Shellfish		**Aguacate** **Alvocat*** Avocado

Soy vegetariano
Sóc vegetarià*
I am a vegetarian

Soy diabético
Sóc diabètic*
I am diabetic

USEFUL NOTES:

_____
_____
_____
_____
_____
_____

60

La cuenta The bill
Lacón Cold shoulder of pork
Lacón con grelos Cold shoulder of porc
with turnip tops
Lado Side
Lagrimitas Pieces
Láminas Slices
Lana Wool
Langosta Rock lobster
Langosta a la catalana Lobster with
mushrooms and ham in a white sauce
Langosta fría con mayonesa Cold lobster
with mayonnaise
Langostinos King prawns
Langostinos con mayonesa King prawns
with mayonnaise
Lanzones Sand eels
Las The
Las sopitas Our soups
Lasaña Lasagne
Lasanya* Lasagne
Laurel Bay leaf
Lecha Soft roe
Lechal Baby lamb
Lechazo milk fed lamb
Leche Milk
Leche frita Pudding with milk and eggs
Leche merengada Cold milk with
meringues
Lechecillas Sweetbreads
Lechón Suckling pig
Lechuga Lettuce

Legumbre Pulse
Lengua Tongue
Lenguado Sole / flounder
Lengua de cordero estofada Stewed lamb
tongue
Lentamente Slowly
Lentejas Lentils
Lentejas aliñadas Lentils with vinaigrette
Libritos de lomo Pork fillet stuffed with
cheese and ham, fried in breadcrumbs
Licuado Liquidized
Liebre Hare
Lima Lime
Limón Lemon
Limpias Clean
Lionesas de nata Profiteroles
Lisa Grey mullet
Llamàntol* Lobster
Llampuga* / daurat* Bream
Llagostí* Prawn / crayfish
Llagostins* Large prawns
Llana* Wool
Llagosta freda amb mayonesa* Cold
lobster with mayonnaise
Llagosta* Rock lobster
Llagosti amb mayonesa* King prawns
with mayonnaise
Llard* Suet
Llauna* Pan (baked in a)
Llavaneres Village near Barcelona
Llavor de rosella* Poppy seed
Llavor de sèsam* Sesame seed

Llebre* Hare
Llegum* Pulse
Lleig* Ugly
Llengua de bacallà* Spanish ling
Llengua de Xai* Stewed lamb tongue
Llengua* Tongue
Llenguado fregit* Fried baby sole
Llenguado* Sole / flounder
Llengeta* Fish similar to whitebait
Llentia* Lentil
Llesca de pa* Slice of bread
Llesca* Slice
Llet* *(pronounced 'yet')* Milk
Lletó* Baby milk
Lletons* Sweetbreads
Lletuga Lettuce
Llimona Lemon
Llissa* Grey mullet
Llobarro* Sea bass
Llom cura* Cured pork sausage
Llom de conill* Saddle of rabbit
Llom de peix* Back of fish
Llom de salteja* Stir fried steak
Llom* Tenderloin
Llombard farcit* Stuffed red cabbage
Llombard saltejat* Sautéed red cabbage
Llombard* Red cabbage
Llonganissa* Pork salami
Llonza* T bone steak
Lloprer* Bay leaf
Llotja* Market
Lluç del riu* Pike

Lluç* Hake
Lluvia* Rain
Lo It
L'olla Pot
Lombardo Red cabbage
Lombardo relleno Stuffed red cabbage
Lombardo salteado Sautéed red cabbage
Lomo Tenderloin
Lomo adobado Marinated pork loin
Lomo curado Cured pork sausage
Lomo de bellota Acorn fed cold meat
Lomo de cerdo Boneless tenderloin
Lomo de conejo Saddle of rabbit
Lomo de pescado Back of fish
Lomo salteado Stir- fried steak
Loncha Slices
Longaniza Pork salami
Los mariscos The shellfish
Los pescados The fish
Lubina Bass
Lubina a la marinera Sea bass in a
parsley sauce
Lubina a la sal Sea bass baked in salt
Lucio Pike
Luvar* Haddock

USEFUL NOTES:

Macarrones Macaroni
Macarrones gratinados Macaroni cheese
Macedonia Fruit salad
Macerado Marinated, salted, matured
Madrileña, a la With tomato, pepper, sausage and paprika
Maduixes amb nata* Strawberries with cream
Maduixa* Strawberry
Madur* Mature / ripe
Magraner* Pomegranate
Magras con tomate Fried ham dipped in tomato sauce
Magre* Lean (usually pork)
Magret Duck breast
Magret de anec* Duck preserved in its own fat
Magret de pato Duck preserved in its own fat
Magro Lean (usually pork)
Mahonesa Mayonnaise
Maíz* Corn
Malonesa Mayonnaise
Mamia Basque junket
Mañana Morning / tomorrow
Manchego Mature cheese
Mandarina Tangerine
Mandongo Black pudding with fennel
Mandonguillas* Meatballs, faggots
Mango Mango
Manises Peanuts
Manitas de cerdo Pigs trotters
Manitas de cordero Lamb shank
Manos de cerdo a la parrilla Char grilled pigs trotters

Mantecado (s) Small sponge cakes
Manteca de res Suet
Mantega* Butter
Mantegada* Ground almond soft biscuit
Mantequilla Butter
Manzana Apple
Manzana silvestre Crab apple
Maó Town in Menorca
Mar Sea
Mar i muntanya* Seafood and meat dish
Maracuya Passion fruit
Maragota Wrasse
Margarina Margarine
Marinado Style of cooking seafood
Mariner* Style of cooking seafood
Marinera Marinade
Marisc* Seafood
Mariscada Mixed shellfish
Marisco Seafood
Mariscos del día Shellfish of the day
Marmita Cooking pot
Marmitako Tuna casserole
Marquesa de chocolate Chocolate mousse
Marró* Brown
Maruca Spanish ling
Masa Pastry, dough
Massapà* Marzipan
Massot* Wrasse
Mata mulo Very fresh
Mató Fresh goats milk cheese
Mazapán Marzipan
Mazorca de maíz Corn on the cob
Mechado Stuffed

Medallones Medallion slice
Medallones de anguila Eel steaks
Medio asado Medium rare
Media ración Medium portion
Mediodía Mid-day / noon
Mejillones Mussels
Mejillones a la marinera Mussels in wine sauce
Mel de canya* Honey from sugar cane
Mel i mató* Cottage cheese and honey
Mel* Honey
Melassa* Treacle
Melaza Treacle
Melindros* Sponge fingers
Melmelada Marmalade
Meló amb pernil* Melon with cured ham
Meló* Melon
Melocotón Peach
Melocotones en almíbar Peaches in syrup
Melón Melon
Melón con jamón Melon with cured ham
Melós* Sticky
Melosa Sticky
Melva Type of tuna fish (smaller)
Melva con morrón Type of tuna fish with red pepper
Membrillo Quince
Mendo limón Lemon sole
Mendrugo Crust
Menestra Vegetable and meat casserole
Menestra de verdures Mixed vegetables
Meniere Sauce
Menjar* Food
Menta* Mint

Menú del dia Fixed price set meal
Menú del pescador Fisherman's menu
Menú sorpresa Menu surprise
Menú turístico Tourist menu
Menudencias Giblets
Menudillos Chicken giblets
Menudo (s) Small / offal
Mercado Market
Mercat* Market
Merenga* Meringue
Merengue Meringue
Merienda Afternoon snack
Merlango Whitting
Merlano Whiting
Merlo Wrasse
Merluza Hake
Merluza a la ondarresa Grilled hake with garlic
Merluza a la riojana Hake with chilli
Mermelada Marmalade
Mermelada de frambuesas Raspberry Jam
Mermelada de fresas Strawberry jam
Mermelada de gerds* Raspberry jam
Mermelada de maduixas* Strawberry jam
Mero Grouper
Mescla* Mixture
Mesón Restaurant (country style)
Mezcla Mixture
Mezclum Mixture
Miel Honey
Mi cuit de pato Duck liver pate
Miel de brezo Honey from flax (wild flowers)
Miel de caña Honey from sugar cane
Miel de maple Maple syrup
Mielga Shark

Migas Breadcrumbs (fried in garlic and other flavours)
Migdia* Mid-day / noon
Mijo Millet
Mil Thousand
Milanesa Cutlet
Milhojas Puff pastry
Mill* Cornmeal bread
Minestra de llegums* Mixed vegetables
Mitjanit* Midnight
Mixta Mixed
Moca Mocha
Moixernon (s) Wild mushroom(s)
Moixó* Small fish / whiting
Mojama Dried tuna
Mojar Wet / dip
Mojo Garlic and hot pepper sauce
Moko Tattoo
Molí* Mill
Molida Ground / crushed
Molino Mill
Moll de roca Red mullet
Moll* Red mullet
Mollejas Sweetbreads
Mollejas fritas de ternera Fried sweetbreads
Mollejas de pollo Chicken gizzards
Mòlt Ground / crushed
Moltó* Mutton
Molusco Mollusc (seafood)
Mongeta* Haricot beans
Mongetes* White beans
Moniato* Sweet potato
Montadito Mini open sandwich
Montado Toasted finger / bread
Montseny Mountain area north of Barcelona

Mora Blackberry / Mulberry
Morcilla Black pudding
Morcilla blana/negra White/black pudding
Morcón Spiced ham / black pudding
Morilla Morels
Moros y cristianos Black beans and rice and garlic
Morralla Small fish / whiting
Morró* Pigs cheek
Morros de cerdo Pigs cheeks
Moradella* Type of salami
Mortadela Type of salami
Moruno (Pinchito Moruno) Small kebab
Morteruelo Type of mince pie
Moscatel Sweet wine
Moscatell* Sweet wine
Mostassa* Mustard
Mostaza Mustard
Motril Town near Malaga
Mousse Mousse
Mousse de chocolate Chocolate mousse
Mousse de limón Lemon mousse
Mullar* Wet / dip
Musaca Moussaka
Musclo* Mussels
Musclos mariners* Mussels in wine sauce
Muselina Muslin cloth
Músic Mixed nuts and sweet wine
Muslo Leg / Thigh
Muslos Mussels
Musola Dog fish
Mussola* Dogfish
Muy condimentado Spicy
Muy hecho Well done

Nabo Turnip
Nabo sueco Swede
Nachos Mexicanos Nachos with spicy sauce
Ñame Yam
Nap* Turnip
Naranja Orange
Naranjada Orange juice
Nata Cream
Nata para batir Whipping cream
Natillas Custard
Natillas de chocolate Cold custard with chocolate
Natillas de la abuela Custard of the house
Natural* Room temperature
Navajas Razor clams
Navarra, a la Stuffed with ham
Navalles* Razor fish
Nécora Small crab
Nectarina Nectarine
Negra (o) Black
Negre* Black
Negritas Chocolate mousse with whipped cream
Nesprer* Sharon fruit
Neteja* Clean
Níscalos Wild mushrooms
Nísperos Sharon fruit
Nit* Night
Noche Evening / night
Ñoquis Gnocchi
Ñora Small dried red peppers

Nostre estil* Our style
Nostres* Ours
Nou Nine
Nou Walnut
Novillo Steer / heifer
Nueces Walnuts
Nuestras Ours
Nuestros asados Our roasts
Nuestro estilo Our style
Nueve Nine
Nuevo, de Again / fresh / new / young
Nue* Walnut
Nuez moscada Nutmeg
Nyam Yam
Nyàmera Jerusalem artichoke

Tips & Helpful Phrases

Catalan words and phrases are identified with an asterisk

Quisiera
Voldria*
I would like or
Tiene
Té*
Do you have

Followed by
Por favor
Si us plau*
Please

Obert* Open
Oca Goose
Oca amb pera* Duck / goose with pears
Oca con peras Duck / goose with pears
Oca* Goose
Ocho Eight
Oli de gira-sol* Sunflower oil
Oli* Olive oil
Oliva* Olive
Oliva (da) Olive (s)
Olivas farcides* Stuffed olives
Olla Pot / stew
Olla gitana Vegetable stew
Olla podrida Soup / stew
Olor Smell
Oloroso Spanish sherry
Opio-nabo Vegetables
Oporto Port
Or* Gold
Orada* Sea bream
Ordi* Barley
Orégano Oregano
Oreja (de Cerdo) Pigs ears
Orejones Dried apricots
Orellana* Dried apricots
Orelletes Fried pastry coated in sugar
Orenga* Oregano
Oro Gold
Ortiga Nettle
Ortiguillas Sea nettle (similar to a jelly
fish)

Orxata* Tiger nut drink
Os de la cama* Leg bone
Os* Bone
Ossobuco Meat on the bone / Italian dish with veal, tomato and garlic sauce
Osteon Oyster
Ostión Scallop
Ostra Oyster
Otoño Autumn
Otro (a) Other
Ou a la mallorquina* Eggs with sausages
Ou dur* Hard boiled egg
Ou ferrat* Fried egg
Ou freigit* Fried egg
Ou (s) Egg (s)
Ous casolans* Home style eggs
Ous de bacallà* Cod roe
Oveja Ewe
Ovella* Ewe, sheep

Tips & Helpful Phrases

Catalan phrases are identified with an asterisk

Nos traería
Ens portaria*
Would you bring us
Estoy bien
Estic bé*
I've had enough (to eat)

Pà cruixent* Crunchy bread
Pà de figues* Dried fig cake with cinnamon
Pà de gingebre* Gingerbread
Pà de pernil* Jellied ham
Pà amb tomàquet* Bread with tomato, oil and garlic spread on it
Pà torrat amb tomàquet* Toast with tomato spread on it
Pà* Bread
Pacana Pecan nut
Padró* Spicy pepper / roll
Padrón Spicy pepper / roll
Paella Rice with chicken and seafood
Paella de bogavante rice dish with lobster
Paella de campiña ice with chicken, bacon and ham
Paella de marisco Rice with shellfish
Paella valenciana Rice with rabbit and chicken
Paella* Frying pan
Pagell* Bream
Pagre* Sea bream
País Country side, local
Paisatge* Country style
Paja Fried potatoes cut into straws
Pajita Straw
Paleta de cordero lechal Shoulder of lamb
Paletilla Shoulder
Palleta* Straw
Palmintos Smoked fish similar to salmon
Palo Éclair
Palo de nata Chocolate éclair

Paloma Pigeon
Palometa Bream
Palomitas Popcorn
Pan Bread
Pan a la Catalana Toasted bread with garlic, tomato and coriander
Pan con tomate Bread with tomato, oil and garlic spread on it
Pan crujiente Crunchy bread
Pan de almendras Bread with almonds
Pan de barra French stick
Pan de higos Dried fig cake with cinnamon
Pan de jengibre Gingerbread
Pan fresco Fresh bread served with olive oil and sherry vinegar
Panaché de fiambres Assorted cold cuts
Pan de jamón Jellied ham
Panache de verduras Vegetable stew
Panaderas Baker
Panadería Bakery
Panadero Baker
Panadés Mallorcan lamb pies
Panadons Pastries
Panceta Streaky bacon / bacon
Panecillo Bread roll
Panera* Basket
Panet* Bread roll
Panquemado Sugar gazed breakfast cereal
Pansa* Raisin
Papa Potatoes
Papas arrugadas Boiled new potatoes

Papel Paper
Paper* Paper
Paperina Ice cream cornet
Paprika Paprika
Para empezar To begin
Para picar To nibble
Pargo Sea bream
Parmesà* Parmesan cheese
Parmesano Parmesan cheese
Parrellada BBQ mixed grill
Parrilla Grilled
Parrillada BBQ mixed grill
Parrillada de caza Mixed grilled game
Parrillada de mariscos Mixed grilled
shellfish
Pasa Raisin
Pasa de Corinto Currant
Pasado Past well done
Pasado por agua Soft boiled
Pasas Raisins
Pasta Dough, pastry
Pasta alimenticia Pasta
Pasta de anchoas Anchovy butter
Pasta de full* Puff pastry
Pasta de sucre i midó* Icing
Pasta fresca Fresh pasta
Pasta italiana Spaghetti
Pasta para rebozar Batter
Pastas Pasta dishes
Pasta quebrada Flaky pastry
Pastada Mash
Pastanaga. Carrot
Pastel Cake, gateau, pie

Pastel de carne Meatloaf
Pastel de chocolate Chocolate cake
Pastel de hígado Liver pâté
Pastel de manzana Apple tart
Pastel de nata Cream cake
Pastel de ternera Veal pie
Pastís* Cake
Pastís amb nata* Cream cake
Pastís de carn* Meatloaf
Pastis de formatge* Cheesecake
Pastís de gelat* Ice cream gateau
Pastís de xocolata* Chocolate cake
Pastís dolç* Sweet tart
Pastor al Shepherd style
Pata Leg / thigh
Patata Potato
Patatas a la Pobre Fried potatoes with onions and red and green peppers
Patatas alioli Potatoes in garlic mayonnaise
Patatas asadas Roast potatoes
Patatas bravas Deep fried potatoes in spicy sauce
Patates fregides *French fries
Patatas fritas French fries
Patatas hervidas Boiled potatoes
Patatas panadera Baked potatoes
Patatas parís Potatoes Paris style
Patatas rellenas Stuffed potatoes
Patatas viudas Potatoes roasted in meat fat
Patatitas Baby potatoes

Paté Paté
Paté de jabugo Paté from acorn fed pig
Pati Skate
Patito Duckling
Patitos rellenos Stuffed duckling
Pato Duck
Pato a la naranja Duck a l'orange
Pato silvestre Wild duck
Pavia Battered fish
Pavo Turkey
Payoyo Goats cheese
Pebre farcit* Stuffed peppers
Pebre* Pepper
Pebros farcits* Red peppers stuffed with
rice, meat or cod
Pebrot* Pepper
Pecho de res Brisket
Pecho curado Corned beef
Pechuga Breast
Pechuga de pollo Chicken breast
Pechuga de pollo rebozada Chicken
breast in batter
Pechuga de Villeroy Breaded chicken fried
Pedir To order
Pedrera* Peppermill
Pedro Ximénez Good sweet sherry
Pedro Ximénez Style With chestnuts, figs
and prunes
Peix espassa* Swordfish
Peix fregit* Fried fish
Peix* Fish
Pela Peel
Pelado Peeled

Pelar To peel
Pelota Large meatball
Pepinillo Gherkin
Pepinillos en vinagreta Gherkins in vinaigrette sauce
Pepino Cucumber
Pepito Steak sandwich / seed
Pequeño (a) Small
Per* For / to
Pera (s) Pear(s)
Perca Perch
Percebes Goose barnacle (crustation)
Percha Perch
Perdices a la campesina Partridges with vegetables
Perdices a al manchega Partridge in red wine with garlic and pepper
Perdigó* Young partridge
Perdigón Young partridge
Perdiu* Partridge
Perdiz (ces) Partridge(s)
Perejil Parsley
Perfectament* Perfect / very good
Perfectamente Perfect / very good
Perlas Baby artichokes
Pernil* Ham
Pernil dolç* Cold boiled ham
Pernil Ibèric* Cured ham
Pernil Serrà* Cured ham
Perretxiku Spring mushrooms
Perrito Hotdog
Perxa* Perch
Pes* Weight

Pescadilla Whiting
Pescadilla Whitebait
Pescaditos Whitebait
Pescado Fish
Pescado frito Fried fish
Peso Weight
Pèsol Pea
Pestiño Honey coated anise flavoured pastry
Pestiños Fried fish
Pètal* Flower petals
Pétalos Flakes / flower petals
Petitó (a)* Small
Petxina de pelegrí* Scallops
Peu* Foot / trotter
Peus de porc a la brasa* Char grilled pigs trotters
Peus de porc* Pigs trotters
Pez Fish
Pez de san pedro John Dory
Pez Espada Swordfish
Pica pica To nibble / mince
Picada To mince / something that thickens a sauce
Picadillo Minced meat / spicy
Picadillo de ternera Chopped cooked veal
Picant* Hot / spicy
Picante Hot / spicy
Picantón Young chicken
Picatoste Croutons
Pichón Young pigeon
Picón Hot spicy sauce
Piel Peel / skin
Pierna Leg / thigh

Pierna deshuesada Boneless leg
Pierna entera T bone
Pies Feet / trotters
Pijama Crème caramel covered in cream served with fruit
Pijotas Fried baby hake
Pilongas Dried chesnuts
Pil pil, al Garlic and parsley green sauce served with fish
Pilotilles* Mounds / balls
Pil-pilando A sizzling dish
Pimentero Peppermill
Pimienta negra Black pepper
Pimienta (o) Pepper
Pimientos asados y aliñados Roast pepper salad
Pimientos rellenos Stuffed peppers
Pimientos a la riojana Red peppers fried in oil and garlic
Pimientos del Piquillo type of pepper
Pimientos verdes Green peppers
Pim-pim Group
Piña Pineapple
Pinchitos Kebab / skewer (tapa)
Pincho Kebab, skewer (tapas)
Pincho Moruno Shish kebab
Pinchón Young pigeon
Pinchos Kebab / skewer
Piñones Pine seeds
Pinsà* Young pigeon
Pintada Guinea fowl
Pinxo* Kebab / skewer
Pinya* Pineapple

Pinyó* Pine seeds
Pinyons* Pine seeds
Pipas Sunflower seeds
Piperita Peppermint
Piperrada Soft creamy omlette in the french style
Piquillo Type of pepper
Piriñaca Salad of mixed chopped vegetables without cucumber
Pirinenc* Pyrenees style
Pirineo Pyrenees style
Pistacho Pistachio nut
Pistatxo* Pistachio nut
Pisto Cooked mixed vegetables
Pisto Manchego Ratatouille
Pit* Breast
Plancha Griddled on a hot plate
Planxa* Griddled on a hot plate
Plat combinat* Mixed plate
Plat* Plate
Plàtan* Banana
Plátano Banana
Platija Plaice
Platillo Small dish
Platillo de pato Stewed duck
Platillo de ternera Veal stew
Platja* Beach
Plato Plate
Platos combinado Mixed plate
Plato principal First course
Plato segundo Second / main course
Plato típico Typical plate
Platos fríos Cold dishes
Playa Beach

Poble* Village
Poblet Village in Catalonia
Pobre* (e) Basic style
Pobre Poor
Pochas Haricot beans
Poc* Not much / little
Pochas Haricot beans
Poco Not much / little
Poleo Type of mint tea
Pollastre amb cava* Chicken with sparkling wine
Pollastre amb tomàquet* Chicken with tomatoes
Pollastre* Chicken
Pollito Young chicken
Pollo Chicken
Pollo al ajillo Fried chicken with garlic
Pollo a la champaña Chicken with sparkling wine
Pollo a la parrilla Grilled chicken
Pollo a la riojana Chicken with peppers and chilli's and wine
Pollo cazadora Hunter style chicken
Pollo con tomate Chicken with tomatoes
Pollo en pepitoria Chicken in wine with saffron garlic and almonds
Polo Ice lolly
Polvorón Ground almond soft biscuit
Poma Apple
Pomelo Grapefruit
Pop a la gallego* Octopus with paprika

Pop* Octopus
Por For
Porc Pig
Porcell / garrí* Suckling pig
Porchella asado Roast suckling pig
Porro* Leek
Porrusalda Leek, mushroom and potato soup
Posada Country restaurant and guest house
Postre Dessert, pudding
Postre del abuelo Fresh cheese with nuts and honey
Postre pepica Special house desert
Pota* Leg / thigh
Potaje Soup / stew
Potaje castellano Thick broth
Potaje de garbanzos Chickpea stew
Potaje de lentejas Lentil stew
Potatge de cigrons* Chickpea stew
Potatge de llentillas* Lentil stew
Potatge* Stew
Pote Hot pot
Praliné Praline
Prat* Meadow
Pre-postre Pre- dessert
Presa Best pork cut
Préssec* Peach
Prima First
Primavera Spring
Primer plat* First course
Primeros First course
Pringadas Bread dipped in olive oil or fat

Profiterol Profiterol
Propina Gratuity / tip
Propuesta del Cheff Chefs special
Pruna* Plum / prune
Prunes* Plum
Puchero Casserole
Puchero canario casserole with chickpeas and corn
Puddin inglés Fruit cake
Pudin (g) Pudding
Pueblo Village
Puercos Pig
Puerro (s) Leeks
Pulpitos Baby octopus
Pulpitos con cebolla Baby octopus with onions
Pulpo Octopus
Pulpo gallega Octopus with paprika
Punta Tip
Puntas de espárragos Asparagus tips
Puntillas Fried small squids
Punxó* On skewers
Pur* Cigar
Puré Mashed / purée
Puré de espinacas Creamed spinach
Puré de garbanzos Hummus
Puré de patatas Mashed potatoes
Puro Cigar
Purrasalda Leeks and potatoes with cod

Quallada* Curd pudding
Quatre* Four
Quemar Brown / burn
Quesada Cheesecake
Queso Cheese
Queso azul Blue cheese
Queso con membrillo Cheese with quince jelly
Queso de Burgos Soft white cheese
Queso de cabra Goats cheese
Queso de oveja Sheep's cheese
Queso de picón Creamy blue cheese
Queso del país Local cheese
Queso emental Dutch emental cheese
Queso frito Fried cheese
Queso Manchego Manchego cheese
Queso Philadelphia Philadelphia cheese
Quetxup* Ketchup
Quisquilla (s) Shrimp

Tips & Helpful Phrases

Catalan words are identified with an asterisk

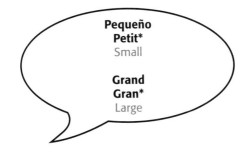

Pequeño
Petit*
Small

Grand
Gran*
Large

Tips & Helpful Phrases

Catalan phrases are identified with an asterisk

No comprendo
No ho entenc*
I do not understand
Habla inglés?
Parla anglès?*
Do you speak English?
Dónde están los servicios por favor?
On estan els serveis, si us plau?*
Where is the toilet please?

Gran variedad de postres a escoger
Gran varietat de postres a escollir*
Assortment of desserts to choose

USEFUL NOTES:

Raba Cod roe
Rábano Radish
Rábano picante Horseradish
Rabo Tail
Rabo de toro Oxtail
Ració* Ration
Ración Ration
Ragout Mixed vegetables and meat
Ragout de ternera Veal ragout
Raïm* Grape
Raja Slice
Rajada* Skate wings
Rallado Grated
Rana Frog
Ranchero Country style
Rancho canario Stew with sausage,
bacon, beans and pasta
Ranci* Stale,rancid
Rancio Stale, rancid
Rap* Monkfish
Rape Monkfish
Rape a la americana White fish with
brandy and herbs
Rape a la cazuela Stewed white fish
Rascacio Rascasse (fish)
Rave* Radish
Raviolis Ravioli
Raya Skate wings
Rebanada de pan Slice of bread
Rebozado Fried in batter

Rebozuelos Wild mushrooms
Recental (al horno) Young suckling animal baked
Recocido Well done
Recubierto Covered
Redondo al horno Roast fillet of beef
Reducción Reduction
Refresc* Soft drinks / refreshments
Refrescos Soft drinks / refreshments
Refritos Stir fried
Regalèssia Liquorice
Regaliz Liquorice
Rehogadas Mixed fry up
Rellena Filled
Relleno(a) Stuffing / filling
Rellenos Stuffed
Remanat* Scrambled egg
Remolacha Beetroot
Remolatxa* Beetroot
Reo Sea trout
Respiro Freshness
Repollo Cabbage
Repostería Selection of small cakes
Repostería de la casa Selection of small cakes (of the house)
Requemado ice pudding with caramelised sugar
Requesón Cottage cheese
Retrete Toilet
Revuelto Scrambled egg
Revuelto de ajos tiernos Scrambled egg with spring garlic

Revuelto de angulas Scrambled egg with baby eels

Revuelto de bacalao Scrambled egg with cod

Revuelto espolón Scrambled egg with prawns

Revuelto de sesos Scrambled egg with brains

Ric* Rich

Rico Rich

Riñon (al jerez) Kidney (s)

Riñones al jerez Kidneys (in sherry)

Rioja Spanish wine

Rioja, a la Rioja style

Riojana, a la With fried chorizo and tomato

Rizada (o) Curl

Robalo Sea bass

Roca Rock

Rodaballo Turbot

Rodaballo salvaje Halibut

Rodaja Slice

Roja (o) Red

Rollito Stuffed cabbage roll / little roll

Rollitos de pescado Fish roll

Rollo de carne Meatloaf

Rollo de primavera Spring roll

Rom* Rum

Romana White wine lemon sauce

Romana a la In batter

Romaní* Rosemary

Romero Rosemary

Romesco Hot sauce made with oil, garlic, peppers and ground nuts

Ron Rum
Ronyó* Kidney
Roquefort Blue cheese
Rosa Pink
Rosca de reyes Pastry filled with candied fruits
Roscas Sweet pastries
Rosegó* Crust
Rosquillas Deep fried ring pastries
Rossejats* Oven baked rice dish
Rossellona* Clams
Rosta Fried bread
Rostir Roast
Rostit* Roast
Roteña Style of Rota
(cooked with veg and tomatoes)
Rovelló* Wild mushrooms
Rovellón Wild mushroom
Royal de chocolate Chocolate cake
Rubio Red gurnard
Ruibarbo Rhubarb
Ruibarbre* Rhubarb
Rus* Russian
Ruso Russian

USEFUL NOTES:

Sabor Taste
Safata* Tray
Safrà* Saffron
Sajolida* Spring onion
Sal Salt
Sal gema Rock salt
Sal marina Sea salt
Saladitos Appetizers
Salchicha Sausage
Salchichas de Frankfurt Frankfurter sausage
Salchichón White sausage with pepper
Salinas Salt marsh
Salmó fumat* Smoked salmon
Salmó* Salmon
Salmón Salmon
Salmón Ahumado Smoked salmon
Salmonete Red Mullet
Salmonetes a la parrilla Grilled red mullet
Salmonetes en papillote Red mullet
cooked in foil
Salmorejo Cold vegetable soup
Salmorra Pickle
Salón Lounge
Saló* Lounge
Salpicón Assortment of meat / Salad with
onions.tomato and peppers
Salpicón de mariscos Shellfish with
vinaigrette
Salsa Sauce
Salsa alioli Mayonnaise with garlic
Salsa almendras Almond sauce
Salsa Americana American dressing

Salsa de ceba* Onion sauce
Salsa de cebolla Onion sauce
Salsa de mora Mulberry sauce
Salsa de tomate Tomato sauce
Salsa Francesa French dressing
Salsa fría Cold dressing
Salsa holandesa Hollandaise sauce
Salsitxa* Sausage
Saltades* Salty
Salteado Sautéed
Saltear Sauté
Salud Cheers
Salut* Cheers
Salvaje Wild
Salvatge Wild
Salvia Sage
Sàlvia* Sage
Sama de pluma Bream
Samfaina* Sauce with tomatoes, peppers,
onions and aubergines
San Jacobo Beef fillet served with ham
and Cheese
San Pedro St Peter's fish
San Pere* St Peter's fish
Sandía Water melon
Sándwich Sandwich
Sangre Congealed blood fried with garlic
Sangría Wine and fruit drink
Sanguina Blood orange
Sanlúcar Place near Cadiz associated with
langoustines
Sard* Bream
Sarsuela de marisc* Seafood casserole
Sarsuela* Seafood stew

Sartén Frying pan
Sashimi Thinly sliced raw
Savarin Sweet desert
Savenna Clams
Sazón (ado) Seasoning (ed)
Sebo Suet
Sec* Dry
Seco Dry
Sègol* Rye
Segons* According to
Según According to
Segundo Second
Seis Six
Seitó* Fresh anchov (ies)
Selección Selection
Semana Week
Semifria Room temperature
Semifred* Room temperature
Semilla Seed
Semilla de ajonjolí Sesame seed
Semilla de alcaravea Caraway seed
Semilla de amapola Poppy seed
Semilla de sésamo Sesame seed
Sémola Semolina
Sèmola* Semolina
Sencer* Whole
Senglar* Wild boar
Señorito Style
Sense* Without
Senyor* Waiter / Mr
Senyoret* Waiter
Sepia Cuttlefish
Sépia amb mandonguilles* Cuttlefish with meatballs
Sepia amb albóndigas Cuttlefish with meatballs

Sepionet* Small squid
Sequillos Hazelnut biscuits
Serie Series
Serrano Cured ham
Servilleta Napkin
Sésamo Sesame
Seso (s) Brains
Sesos a la romana Fried lambs brains in batter
Seta Wild mushroom
Setas a la segoviana Mushrooms segoviana style
Setas de cardo Oyster mushrooms
Setas rellenas Stuffed mushrooms
Sèu* Suet
Si us plau* Please
Sidra Cider
Siete Seven
Siguienta Following / next
Silla Chair
Silvestre Wild
Sin Without
Sin piel Peeled
Síndria* Watermelon
Sinfonía Symphony
Sípia* Cuttlefish
Sis Six
Sobrasada Spicy red sausage from Mallorca
Sobre Upon / over
Sòcol* On a bed of
Sofregit* Fried with olive oil, garlic and tomatoes
Sofrito Fried with olive oil, garlic and tomatoes

Solla Plaice
Solé Single
Solo Single / sole
Solomillo Sirloin
Solomillo a la parrilla Grilled steak
Solomillo con guisantes Fillet steak with peas
Solomillo con patatas Fillet steak with potatoes
Solomillo de ternera Fillet of veal
Sonso* Sand eels
Sonsos Sand eels
Sopa Soup
Sopa castellana Vegetable / Garlic soup
Sopa clara Clear soup
Sopa de ajo Garlic soup
Sopa d'all* Garlic soup / could be chilled
Sopa de almendros Almond based pudding
Sopa de Calabaza Pumpkin Soup
Sopa de cangrejos Crab bisque
Sopa de cocido Watery meat soup
Sopa de cranc* Crab soup
Sopa de muscles* Seafood soup
Sopa de mariscos Seafood soup
Sopa de mejillones Mussel soup
Sopa de peix* Fish soup
Sopa de pescado Fish soup
Sopa del día Soup of the day
Sorbet* Sorbet
Sorbete Sorbet
Sortint* Projecting
Sota* Under
Soto Grove / thicket
Soufflé Soufflé
Soufflé de fresones Strawberry soufflé

Soufflé de queso Cheese soufflé
Spaetzle alsacianas Noodles (from Alsace)
Spaghetti Napolitana Spaghetti in tomato and herb sauce
Steak tartar Steak tatare (minced beef which is eaten raw)
Stic Steak
Stik Steak
Suau* Gentle / smooth / soft
Suave Gentle / smooth / soft
Suc de llima* Lime juice
Suc de Llimona* Lemon juice
Suc de pressec* Peach juice
Suc de tomàquet* Tomato juice
Suc natural* Fresh fruit juice
Suc Juice / squash
Sucre* Sugar
Suficient Enough
Suflé Soufflé
Sumlement* Additional / extra
Suplemento Additional, extra
Suplemento de verduras Extra vegetables
Supremas de pescado Fish supremes
Suro* Cork
Surtido Platter / assortment
Surtido alarifes Assorted desserts
Surtido de embutidos Assorted cold sausage and salami
Surtido de fiambres Assorted cold meats
Surtido de quesos Assorted cheese platter
Sushi Japanese presentation of sea food

Tabla Platter / assortment
Tabla de embutidos Assorted cold
sausages and salamis
Tabla de quesos Assorted cheese platter
Taco Thin pastry wrap
Tacs* Small pieces
Tajada Slice
Talada Slice
Tall rodó* Cut of meat
Tallarines Noodles
Tallarines a la italiana Tagliatelle
Tallat* Expresso with a drop of milk
Tamarinde Tamarind
Tamarindo Tamarind
Tambor Drum
Tancat* Closed
Tapas Spanish appetizer
Tapenade Olive and anchovy paste
Tàpera Capers
Tapitas Appetizers
Tarde Evening / afternoon
Tardor* Autumn
Taronja Orange
Tarta con crema Cream cake
Tarta de almendra Almond tart
Tarta de chocolate Chocolate tart
Tarta de helado Ice cream gateau
Tarta de queso Cheesecake
Tarta dulce Sweet tart
Tarta Romántica Ice cream cake
Tarta selene Type of tart
Tarta tatin Tart
Tartalea Tart
Tartar Tartare
Tártara Cake / tart

Tassa Cup
Taul Plate / assortment
Taula de embotits* Assorted cold sausage and salami
Taula de formatees* Cheese platter
Tauró* Shark
Taza Cup
Tazón Bowl
Té Tea
Te amb llimona* Lemon tea
Té con limon Lemon tea
Tebi Warm
Tejas Almond and sugar biscuits
Tejocote Crab apple
Telina* Wedge shell clam
Tellinas Wedge shell clam
Pemperat* Warm
Templada Warm
Temporada Time / Season
Tempranillo Young wine
Temptació* Temptation
Tencas Tench
Tendre* Ripe / Tender
Tenedor Fork
Tentación Temptation
Ternasco Baby lamb
Ternasco asado Roast baby lamb
Ternera Beef
Ternera asada Roast veal
Terrina de foie Cold paté
Terrina de foie amb mermelade de figues Paté cake with fig marmalade
Terrina de foie con mermelada de hijos Paté cake with fig marmelade
Tibio Warm

Tiburón Shark
Tiempo Of the season
Tierno (a) Ripe / Tender
Tiernos Tender
Timbal Fruit pudding
Tinta, en su In its own ink
Tinto de verano Chilled red wine
Típicas Typical
Tirabeque Mangetout
Tiramisur Tiramisu
Tiras Strips
Tires* Strips
Tocino Bacon
Tocino de cielo Rich egg and syrup dessert
similar to crème caramel
Tòfona* Truffle
Tófono Tofu
Tomàquet* Tomato
Tomàquets farcits* Stuffed tomatoes
Tomate Tomato
Tomates rellenos Stuffed tomatoes
Tomillo Thyme
Tonyina* Tuna
Tord* Thrush
Tordo Thrush
Tornedo Tenderloin
Toro Bull
Toronja Grapefruit
Torre Tower
Torre* Tower
Torrijas Sweet pastries eaten at Easter
Torró Type of nougat
Torta Sponge cake
Torrada Toast
Tortilla Omelette

Tortilla a la paisana Omelette with vegetables

Tortilla su gusto Omelette made to the customers wishes

Tortilla Alaska Baked Alaska

Tortilla Española Thick fried potato omelette

Tortilla de camarone Marinated grouper and prawn omelette

Tortilla francesca Plain omelette (french)

Tortilla sacramente Vegetable, brain and sausage omelette

Tortilla variada Varied omlette

Tortillitas Fritters

Tortuga Turtle

Tostaditas Small pieces of toast

Tostado Toasted

Tostones Fried bread

Tou* Soft / bland

Tournedo Tenderloin

Toyina Salted tuna

Tradicional Traditional

Traguet* Drink

Trancha Slice (french)

Trencadissa* Brittle / fragile

Tres Three

Tria* Choose / select

Trigo Wheat

Trigueros Green asparagus

Trinxat* Bubble and squeak with bacon

Tripa Tripe

Triturado Shreaded / crushed

Triturat* Shreaded / crushed

Troceado Chopped

Tronc* Trunk / body

Tronco Trunk / body
Tronco de merluza Baked hake
Tropezones Large chunks
Tropiezos Chunks / garnish
Tros* Piece
Trossejat* Chopped
Trozo Piece
Trucha a la Navarra Trout cooked with ham
Trucha ahumada Smoked trout
Trucha escabechada Marinated trout
Trucha marina Sea trout
Truchas Trout
Trufa (s) Truffle
Truita de patata* Thick fried potato omelette
Truita escabetxada* Marinated trout
Truita a la fransesa* Plain omelette (french)
Truita fumat* Smoked trout
Truita* Omelette
Truita* Trout
Tu You
Tubo Small beer / tube / pipe
Tuc* Top / apex
Tudela Town near Pomplana / Type of lettuce / asparagus
Tuétano Bone marrow
Tupa Stuffing / filling
Turbot* Turbot
Turrón Type of nougat
Txakolí Basque wine
Txalotas Shallots
Txipiron* Baby squid

Tips & Helpful Phrases

Hola
Hello
Adiós
Adéu*
Goodbye

Buenos días
Bon dia*
Good morning
Buenas tardes
Bona tarda*
Good afternoon
Buenas noches
Bona nit*
Good evening

USEFUL NOTES:

Ubre de vaca Cows udder
Un A or an
Unidad Unit / piece
Unitat* Unit / piece
Uno One
Untar Spread
Untar con mantequilla Spread with butter
Urta (s) Fish
Uva (s) Grape

USEFUL NOTES:

Tips & Helpful Phrases

Con,
Amb*
With
Sin,
Sense*
Without

Bien hecho / bien asado
Ben fet*
Well done
Medio asado
Al punt*
Medium
Poco hecho
Poc fet*
Rare
Del país
Local

USEFUL NOTES:

Vaca Cow
Vaina Pod
Vainilla Vanilla
Vapor Steam
Variado Assorted
Vasca (ala) Basque style
Vasito Small glass
Vaso Glass
Vedella* Beef
Vegetal Vegetable
Vegetales Vegetables
Vegetariano Vegetarian
Vell, anyenc Aged / old
Venado Venison
Venao Venison
Ventall* Something displayed on a tray
Ventr* Belly
Ventresca Cut of fish
Verano Summer
Verd* Green
Verde Green
Verdura Boiled vegetables
Verduras al vapor Steamed vegetables
Verduritas Small vegetables
Vesprada* Evening
Vespre* Evening / afternoon
Vi Wine
Viandes Food
Viejo Old / mature
Vientre Belly
Viera (s) Scallops
Vilajuiga Wine

Vilanova Town / Style of cooking
Villeroy Town / style of cooking
Víña Wine
Vinagre Vinegar
Vinagreta French dressing
Vino Wine
Vino tino Red wine
Vinya Vine
Virutas Shavings
Virutas de jamón Thin and small slices of ham
Vuelta y vuelta Rare

Acknowledgement

Thanks to Monica Taylor, Raquel Iglesias Maellas, Holly Sutcliffe, Maureen McDonnell, Amelia Jackson and Mark Redsell all of whom have helped me with the publication of this book.

Whisky Whisky

Xai* Lamb
Xarop* Syrup
Xató* Green salad with salt cod
Xocolata Chocolate

Y And
Yema Yolk
Yema de huevo Egg yolks
Yogur Yoghurt
Yogur de fruta Fruit yoghurt

Zalbichada (con) Dried nuts sauce
Zanahorias Carrots
Zanahorias a la crema Carrots in cream
Zancarrón Black pudding from Cantabria
Zarajos Fried lambs intestines
Zarzamora Blackberry
Zarzuela Seafood stew
Zarzuela de mariscos Seafood casserole
Zocalo Filling
Zona Area
Zorza Fried pork with paprika
Zumo Juice
Zumo de melocotón Peach juice
Zumo de tomate Tomato juice
Zumo natural Fresh fruit juice